I0481877

Coloring Book

OWLS

First Edition

Distributed by : CreateSpace

ISBN-13: 978-1984224064

ISBN-10: 1984224069

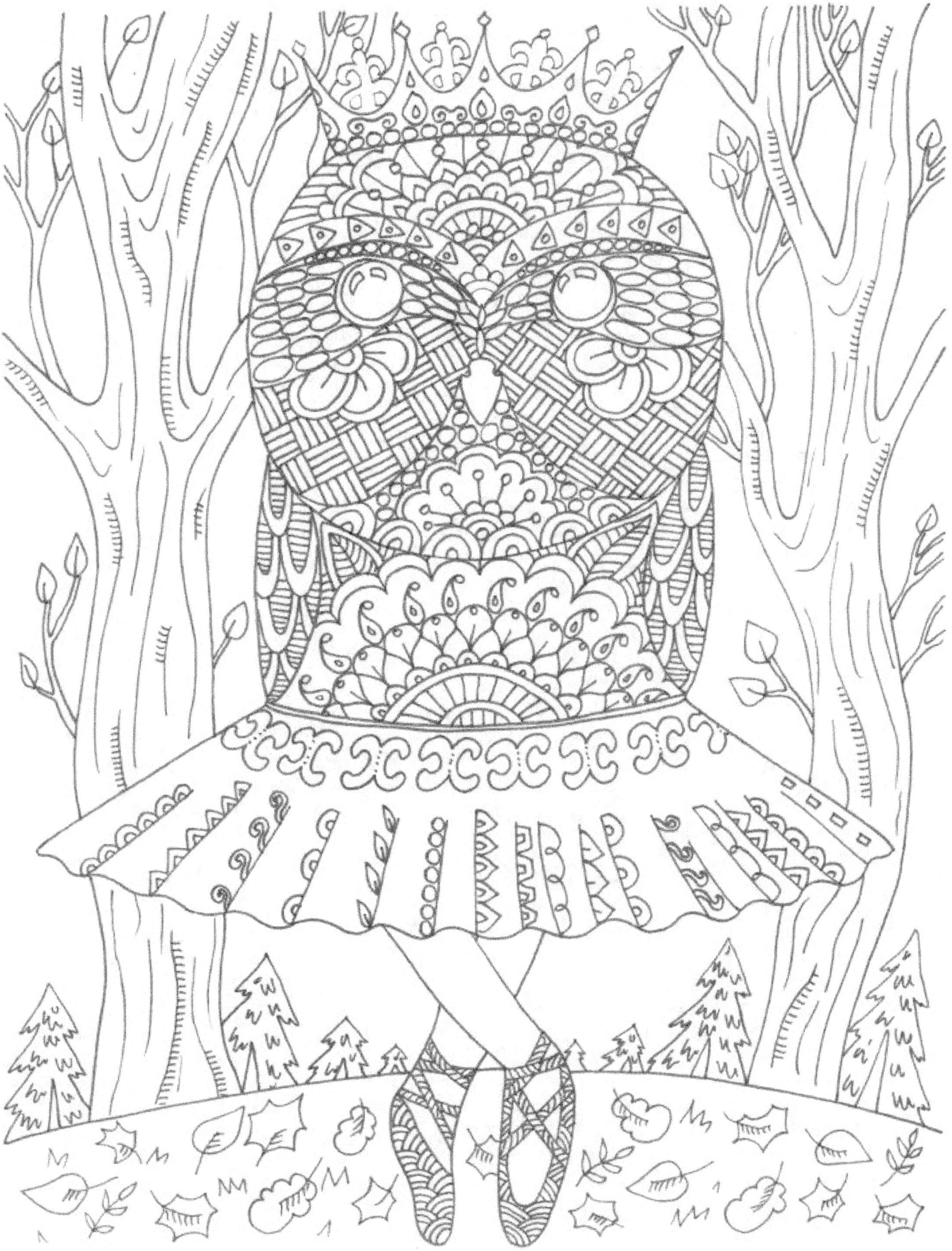

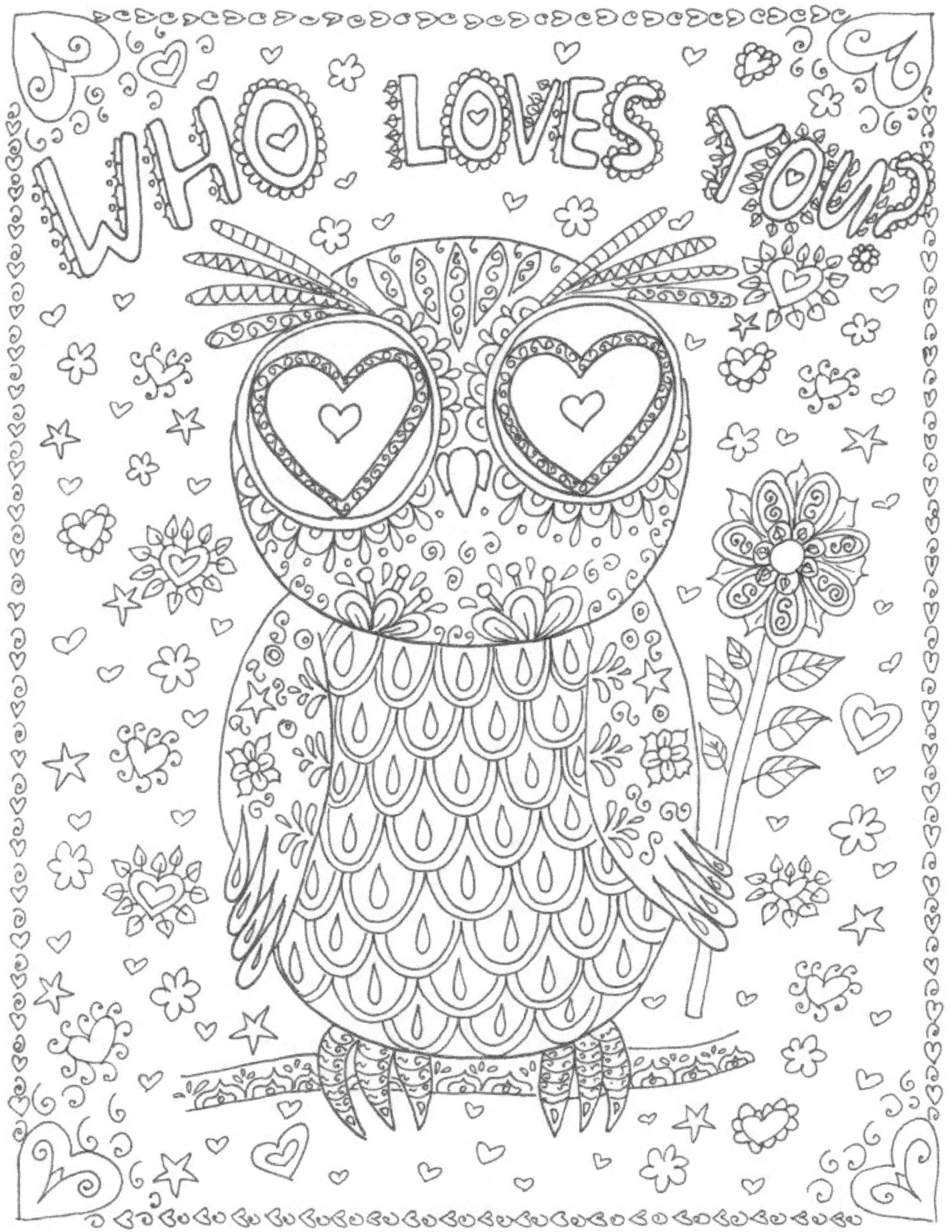
WHO LOVES YOU?

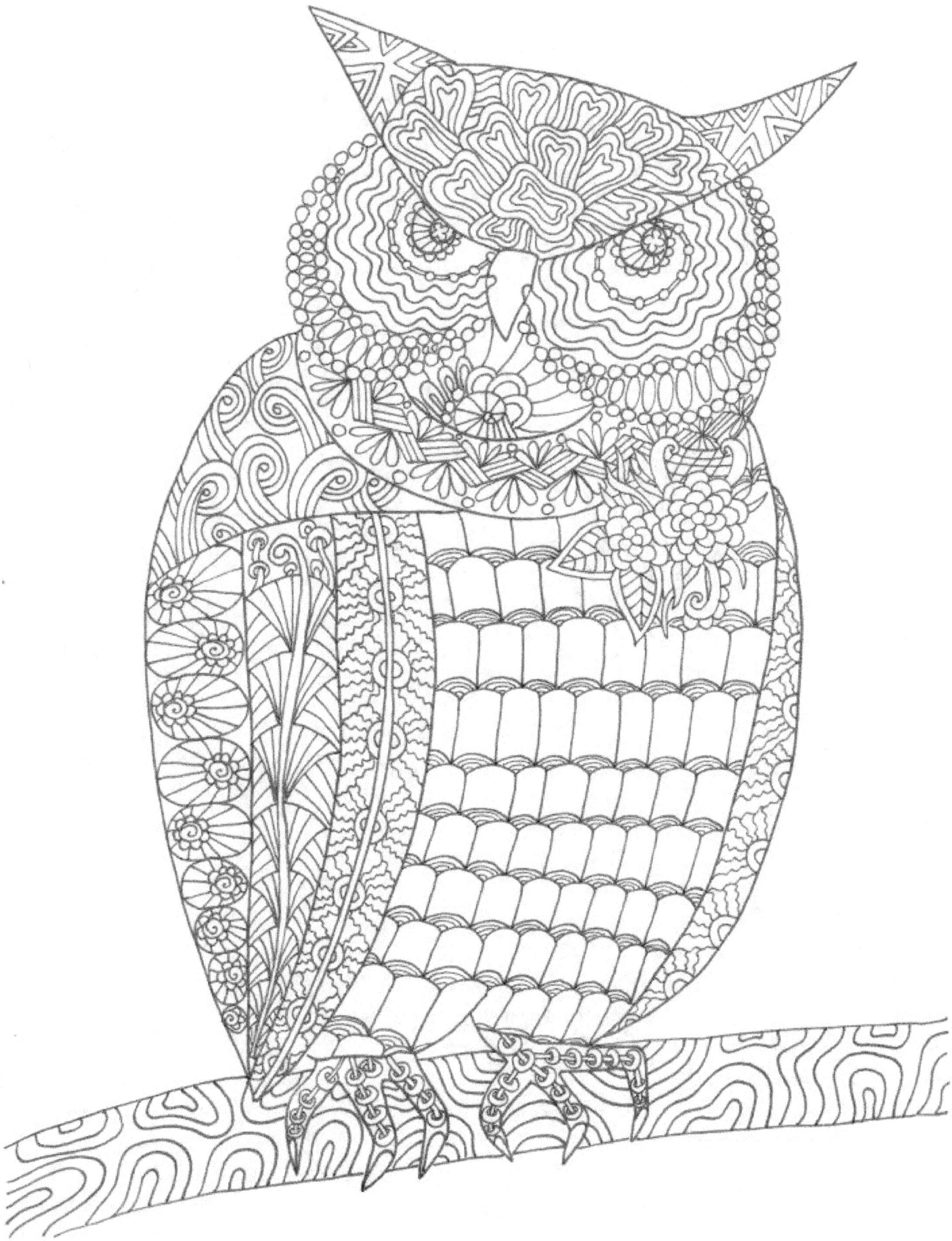

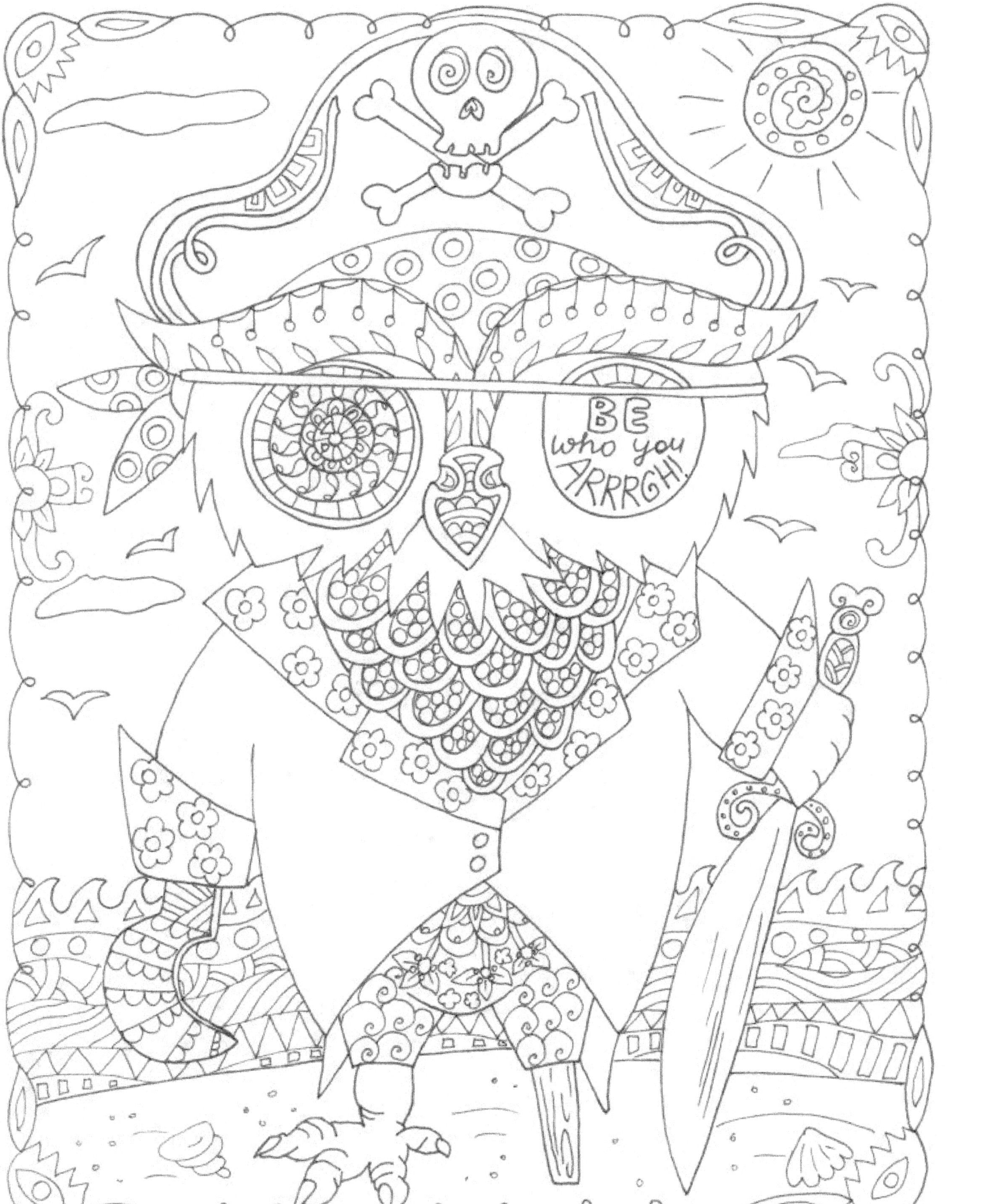
BE
who you
ARRRGH!

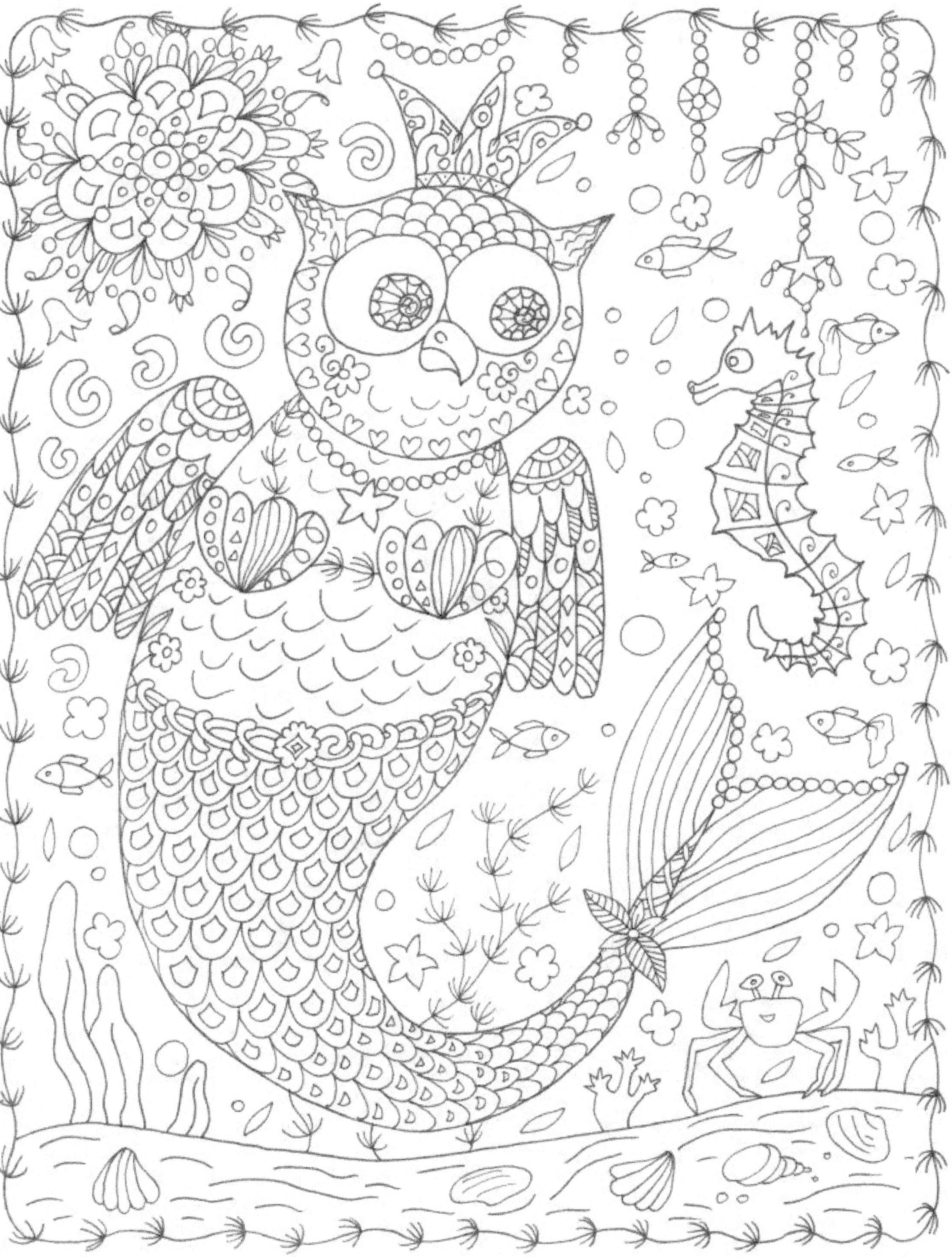

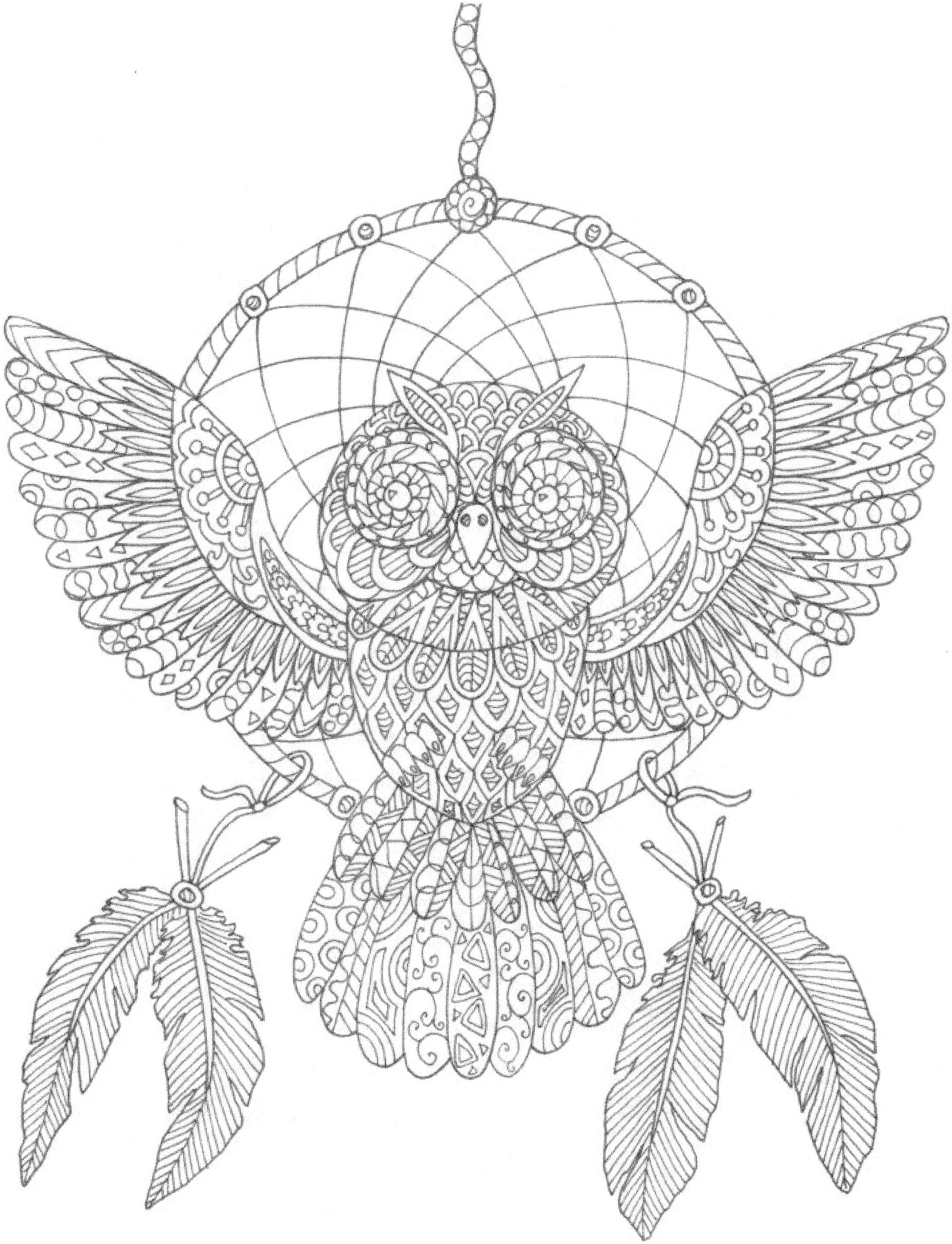

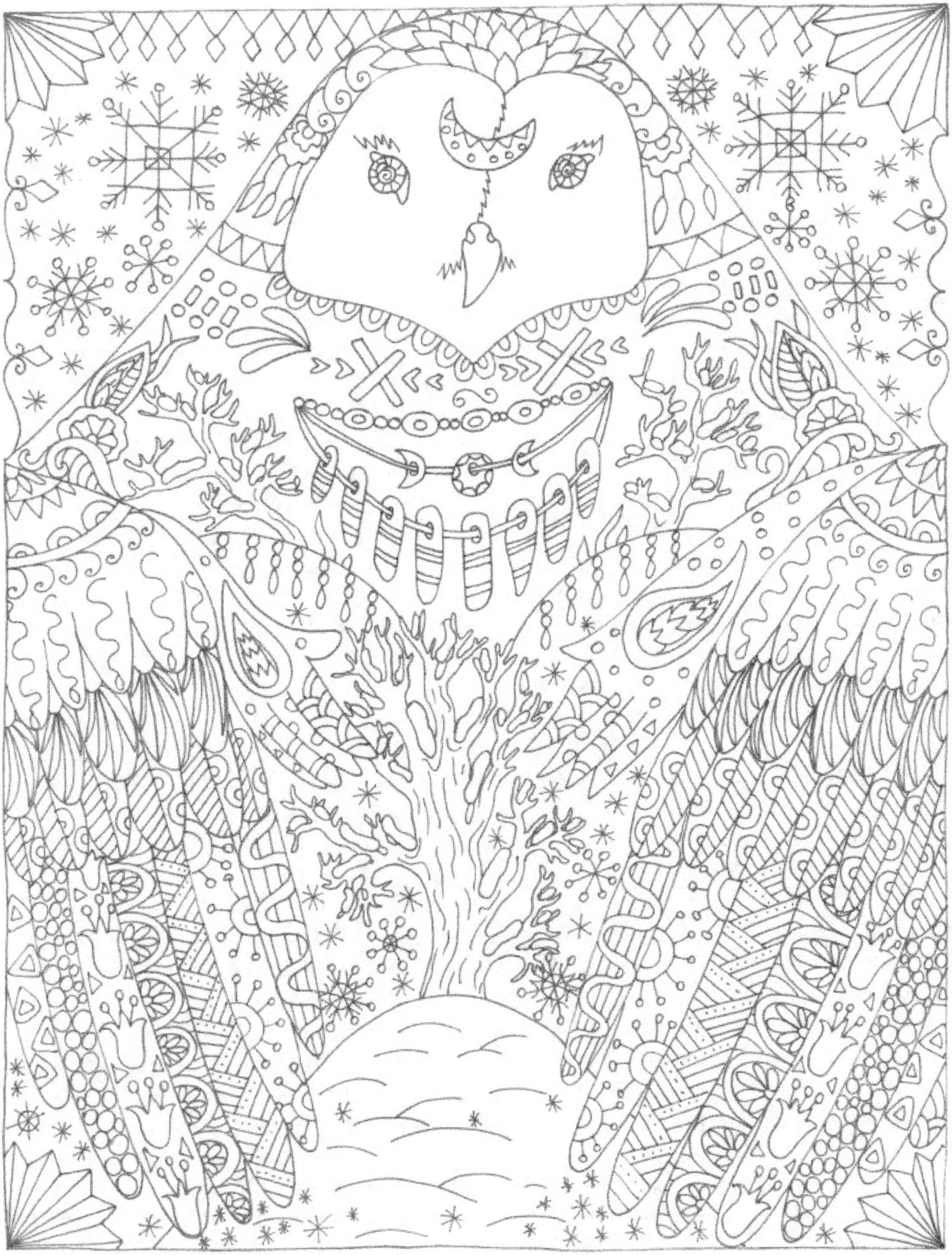

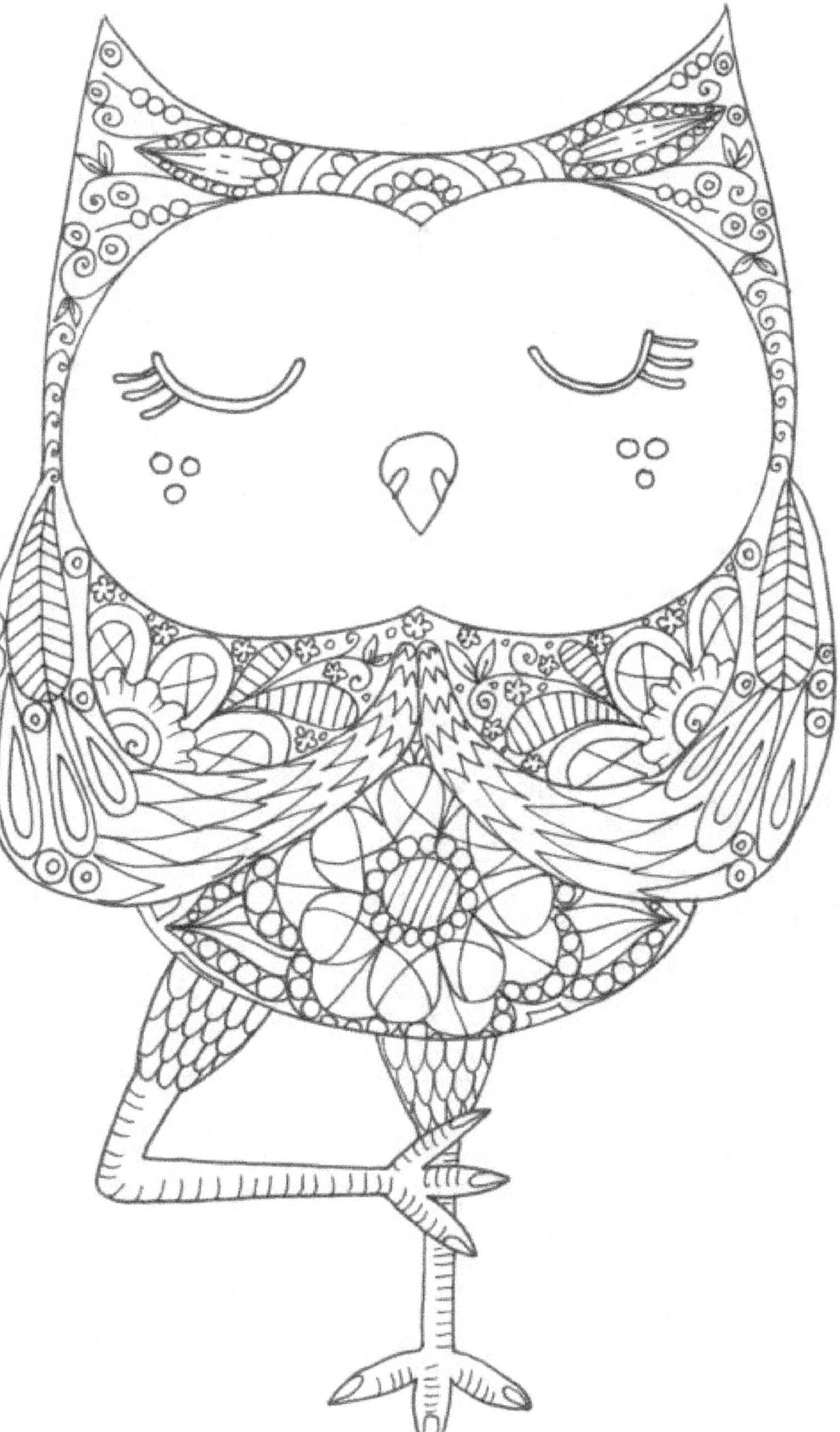

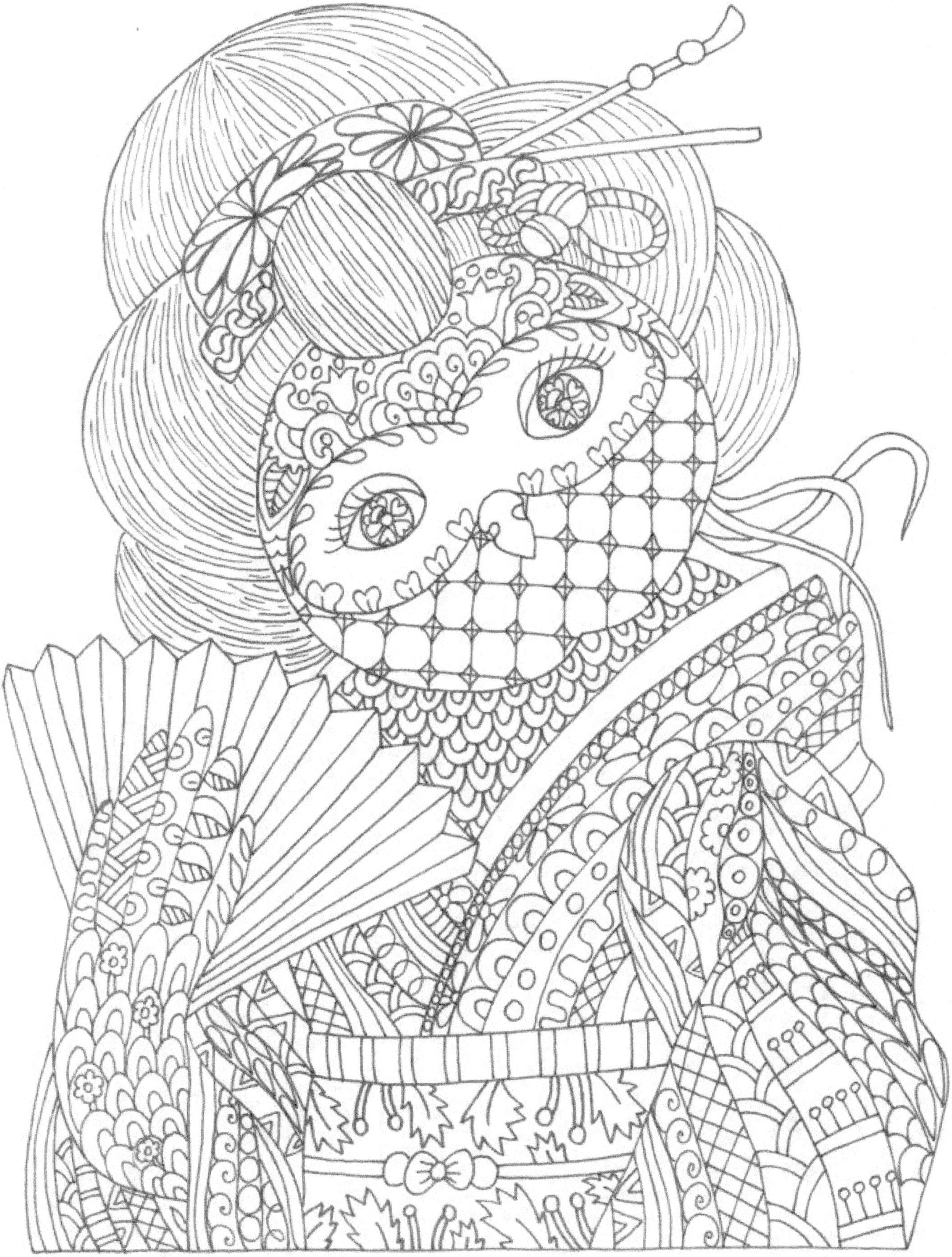

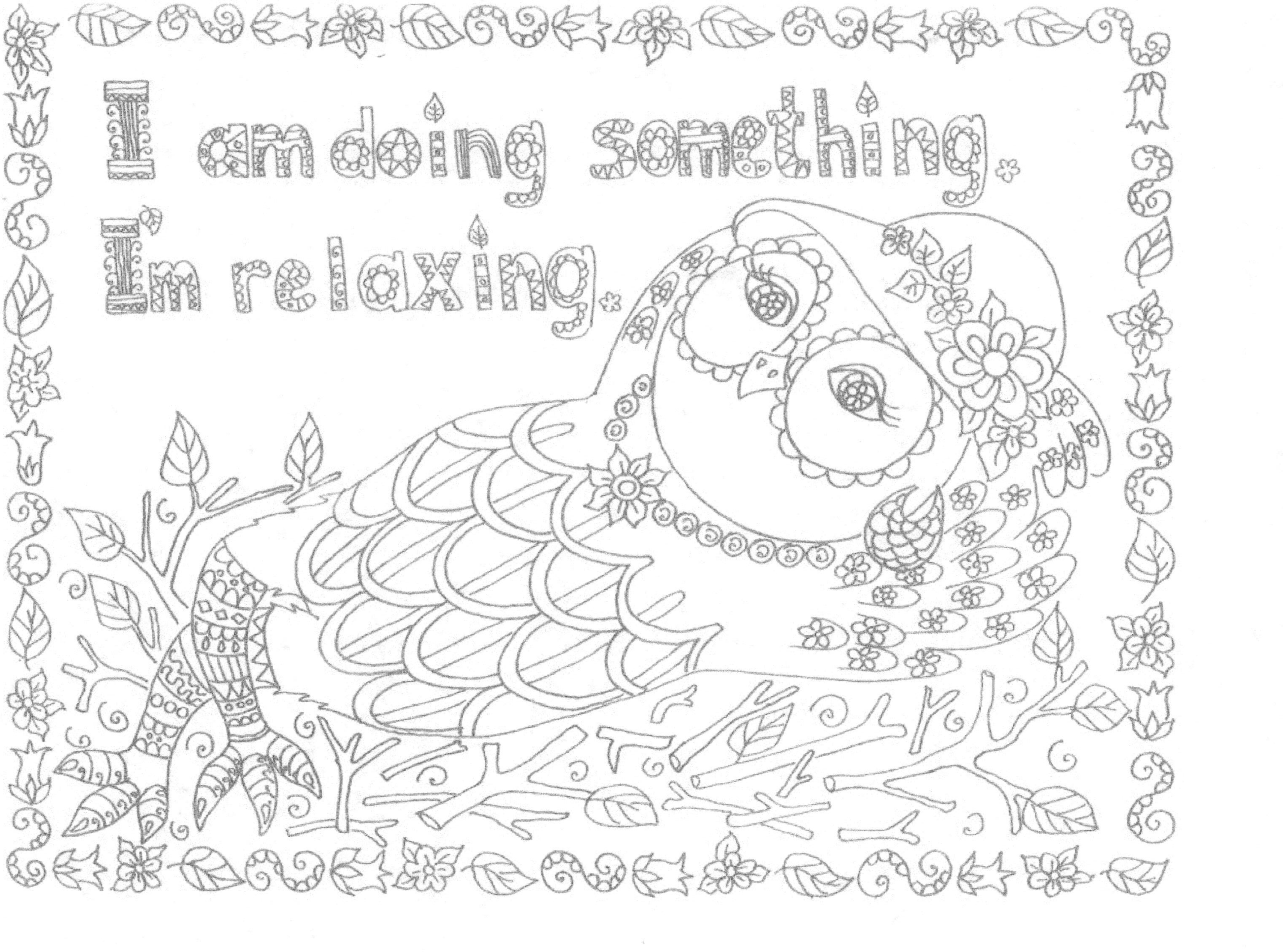
I am doing something.
I'm relaxing.

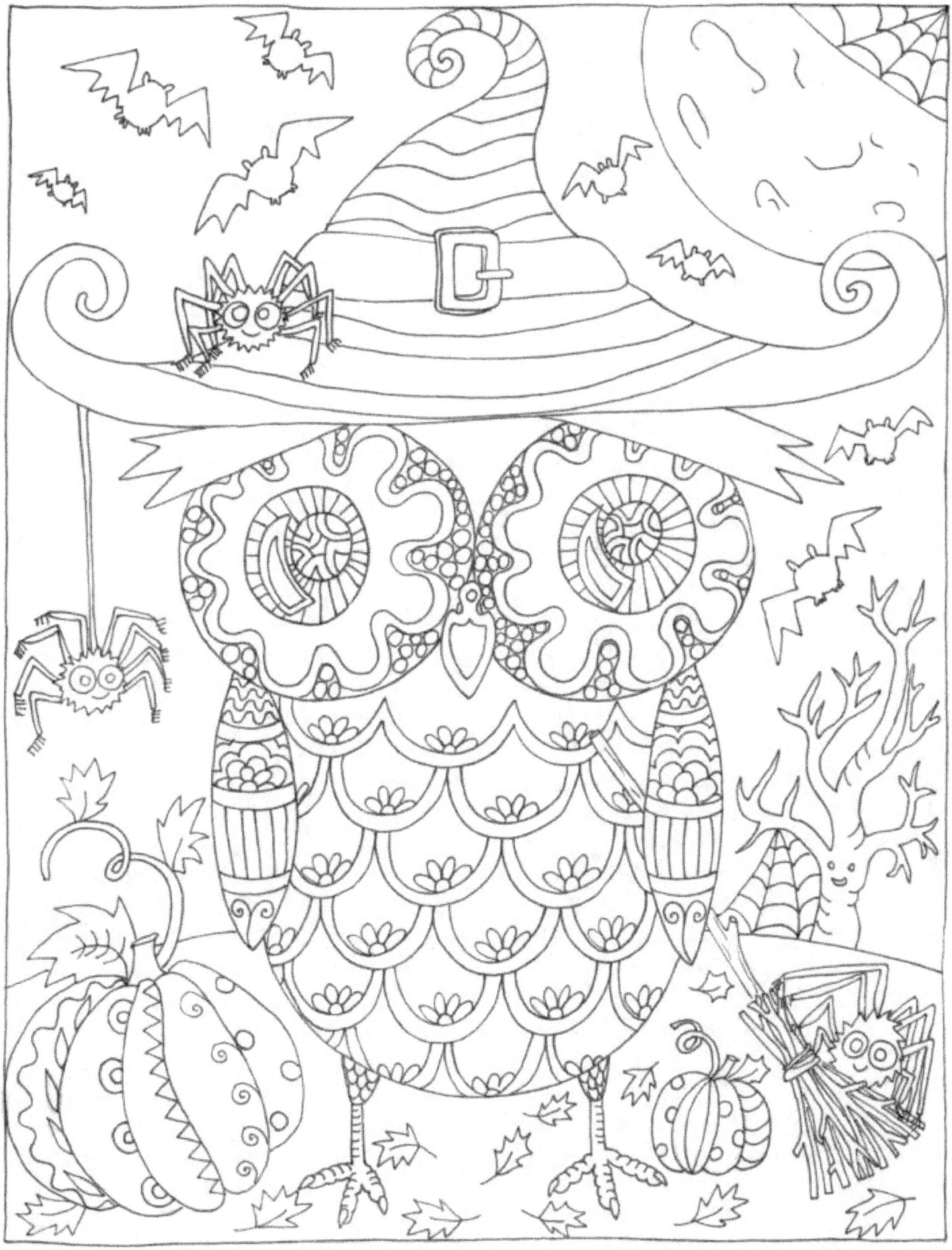

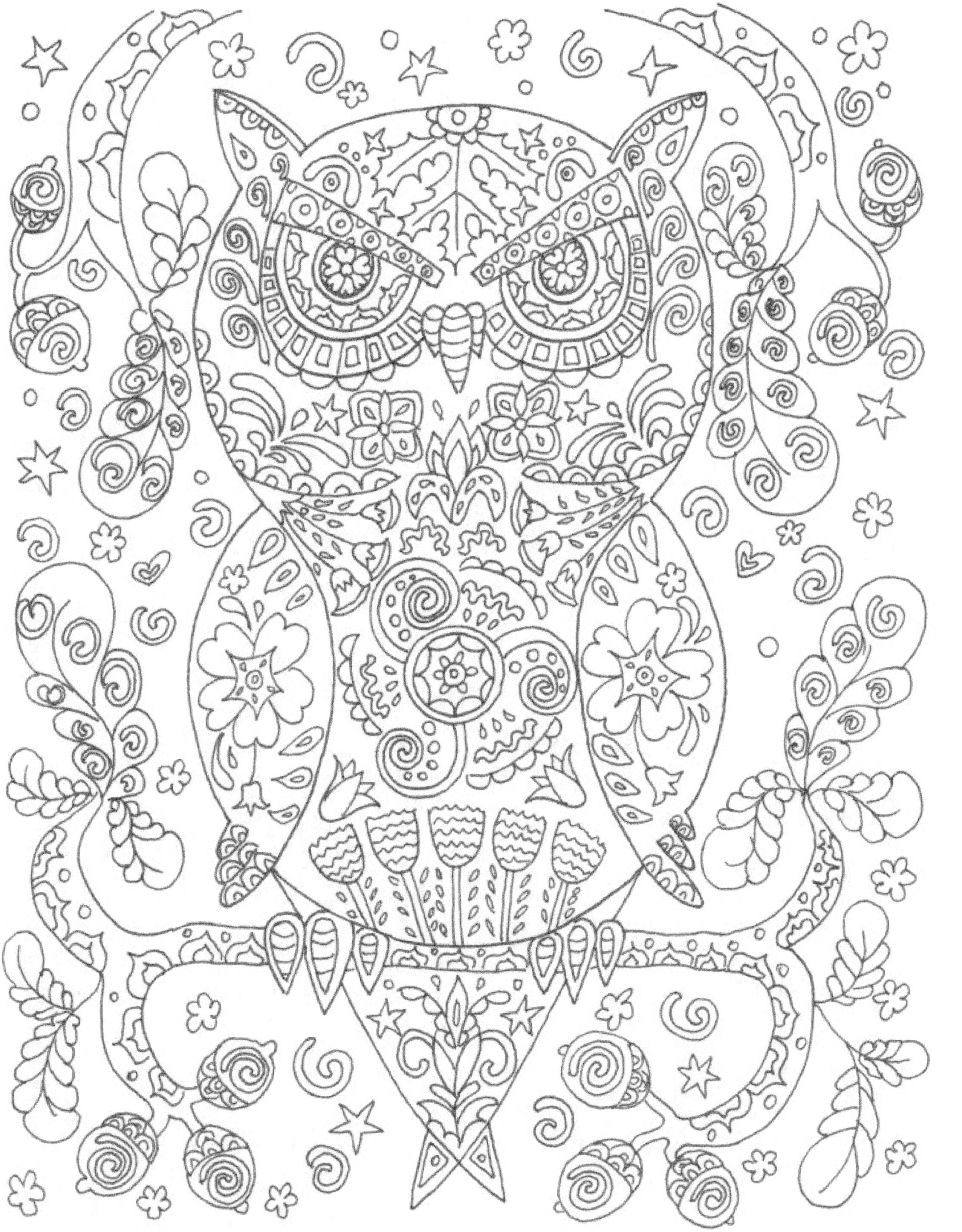

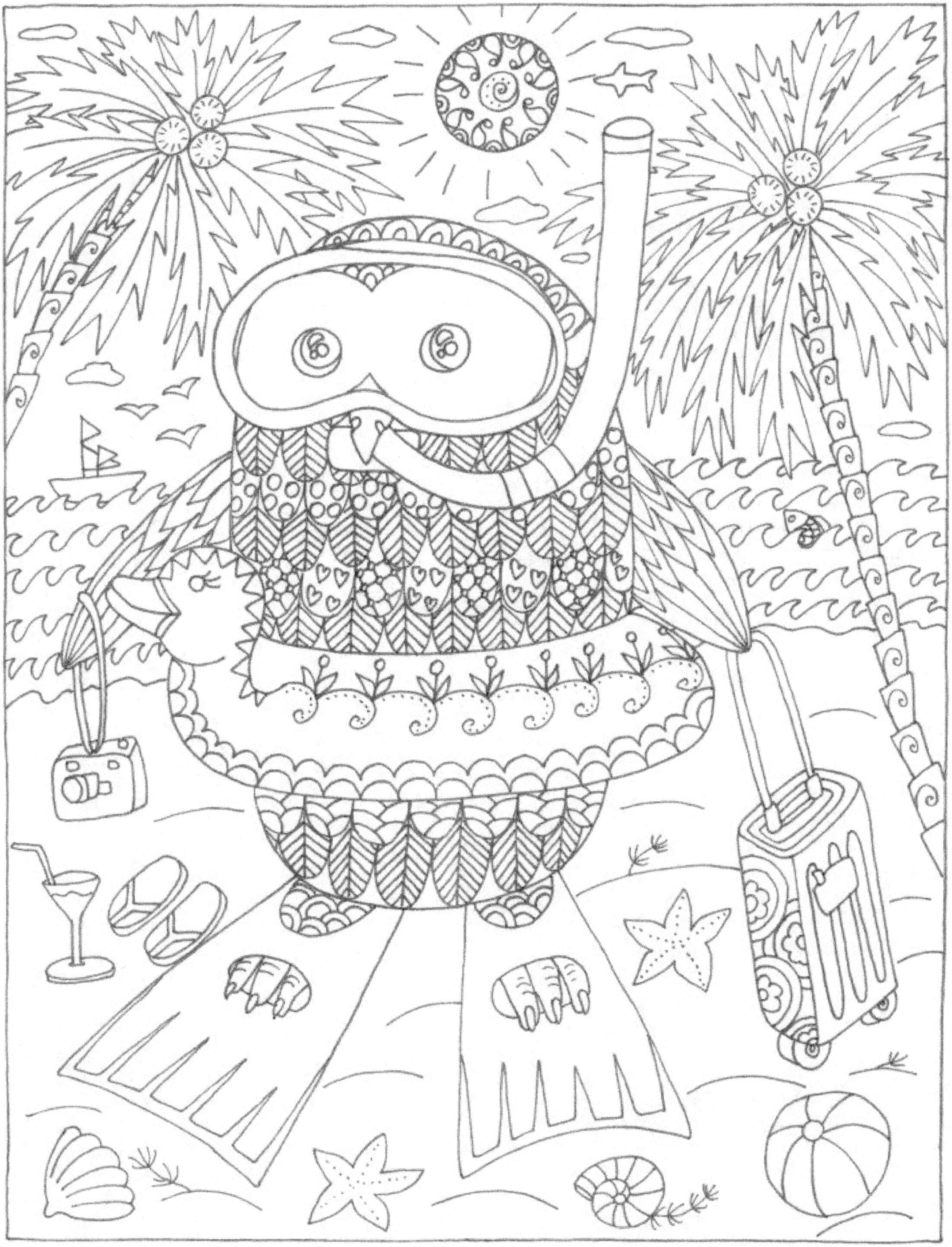

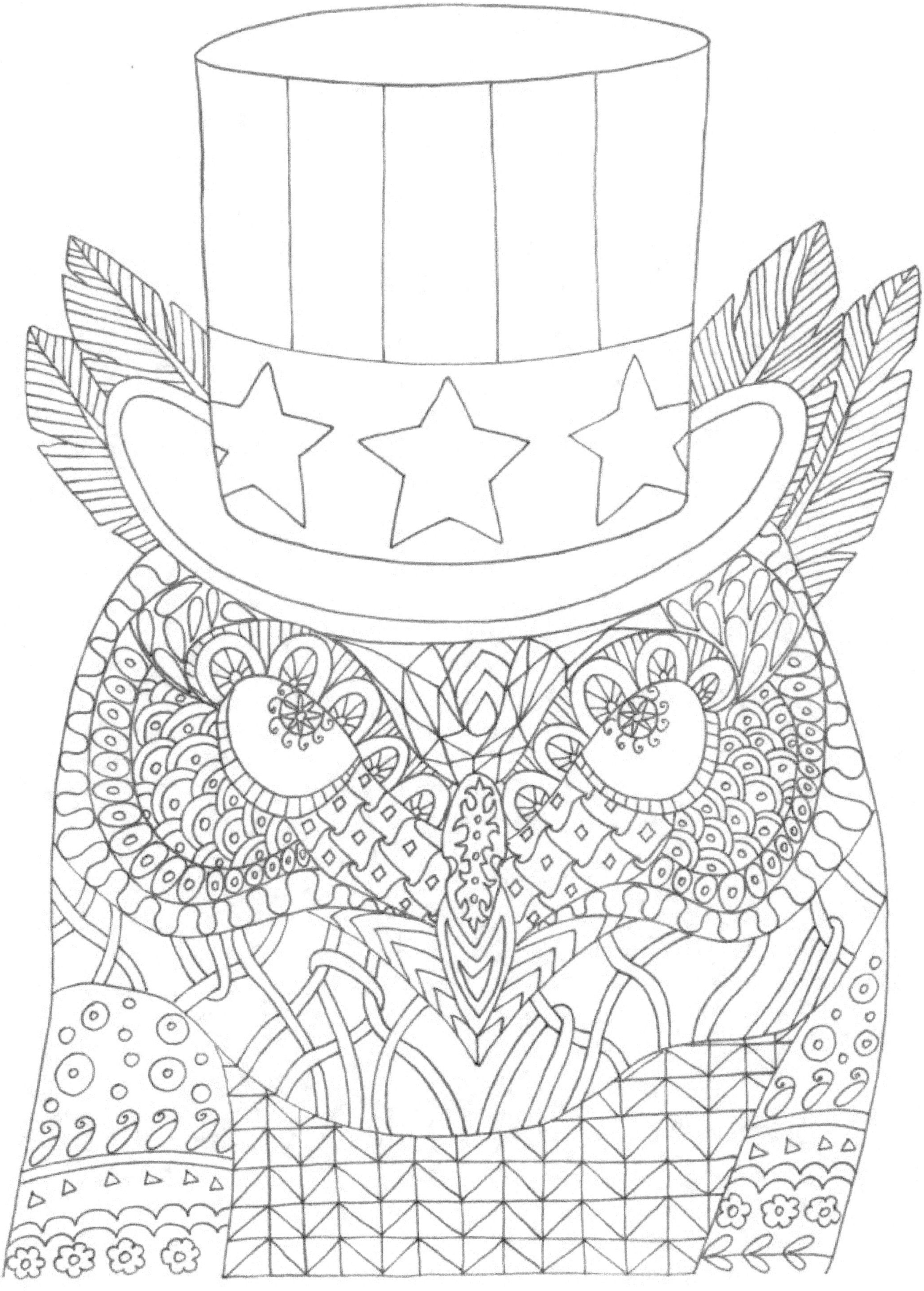

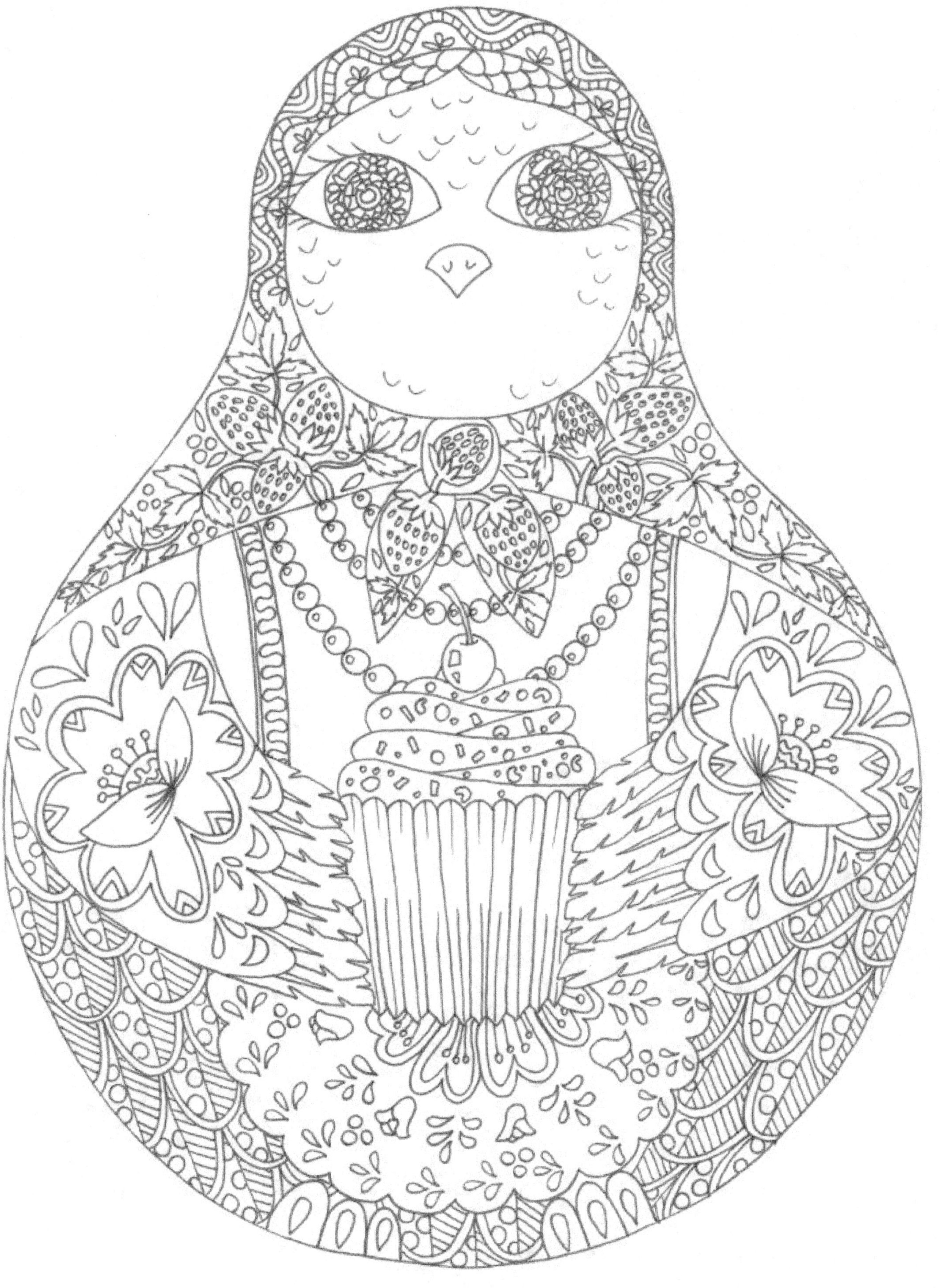

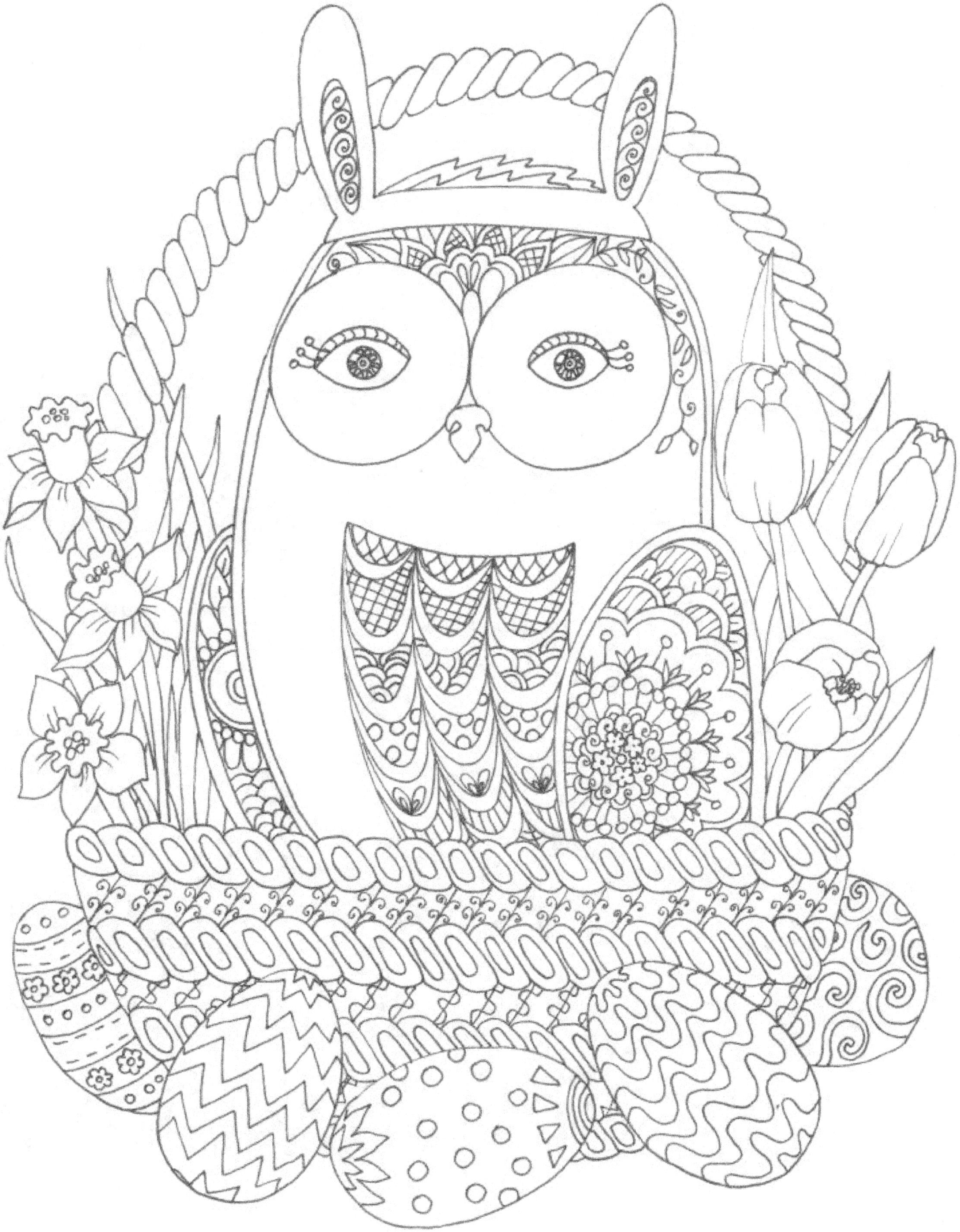

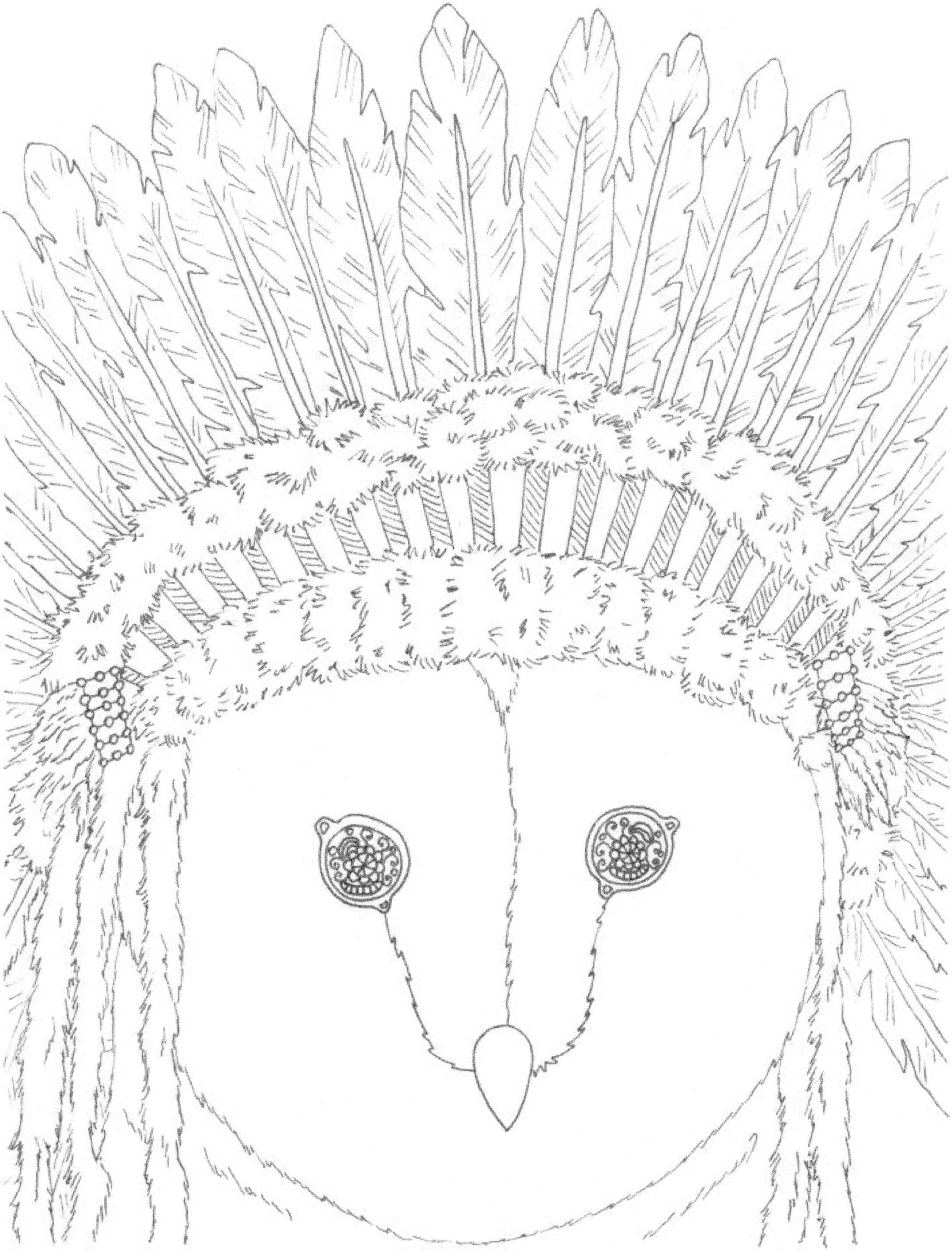

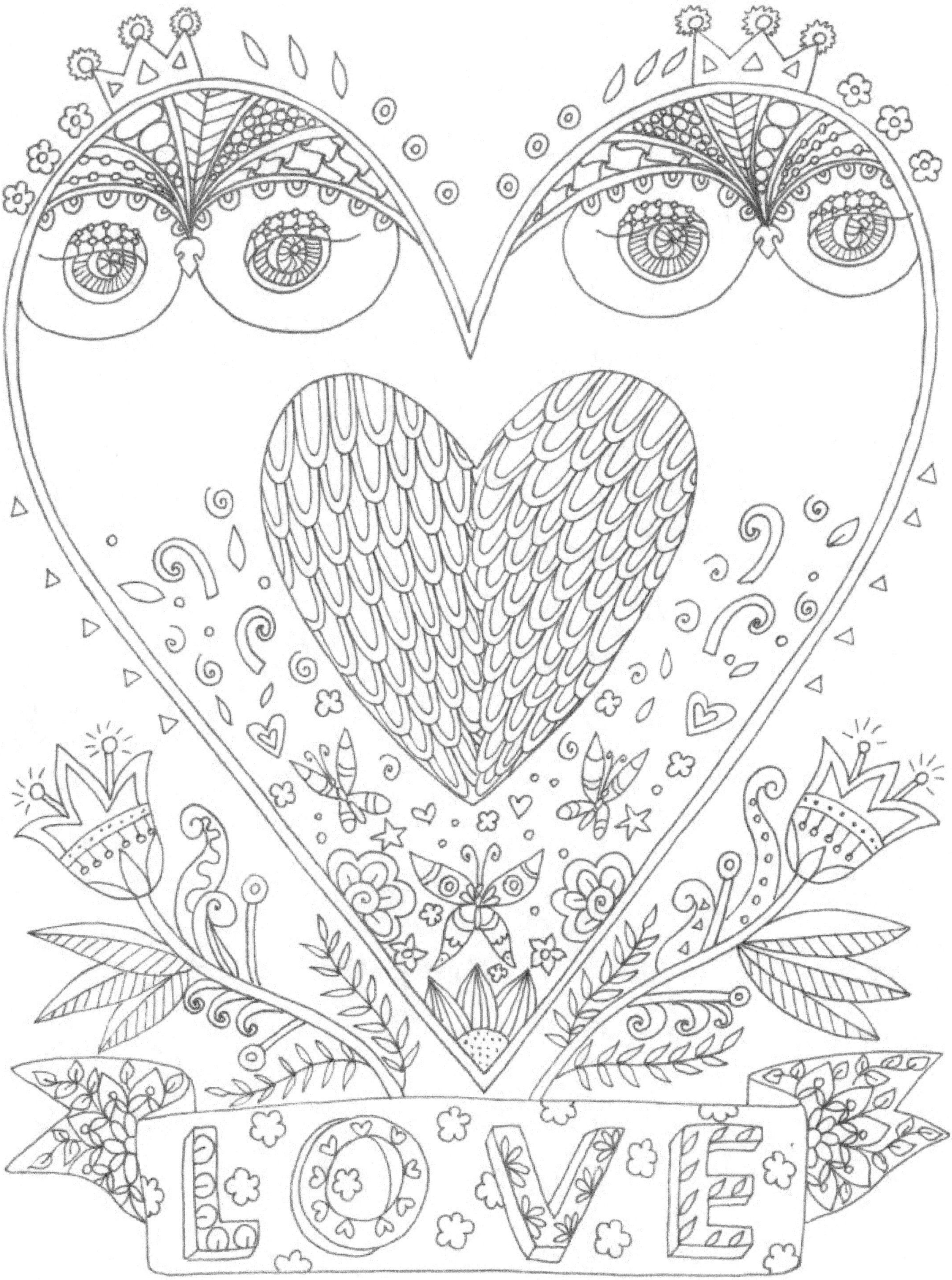
LOVE

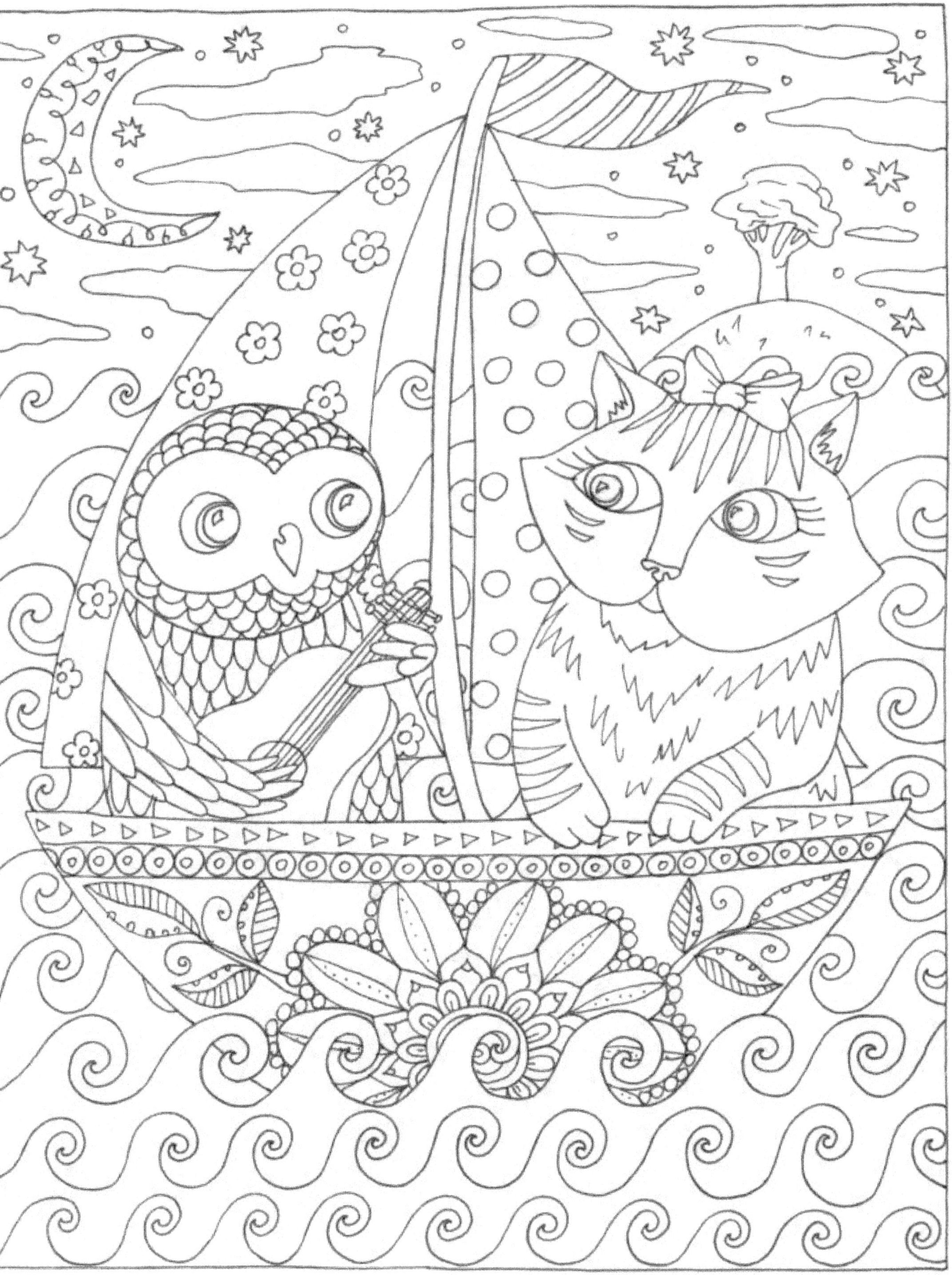

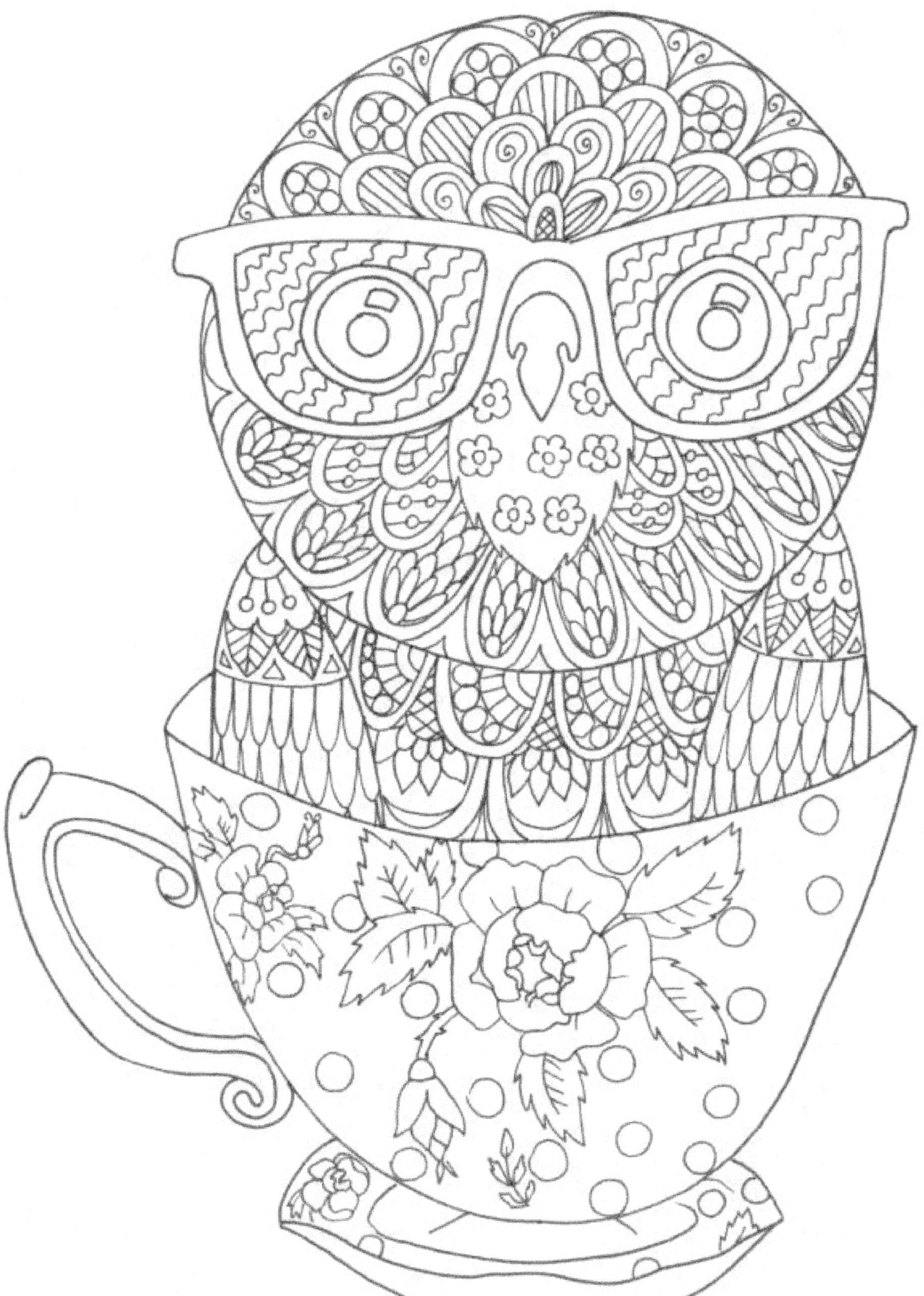

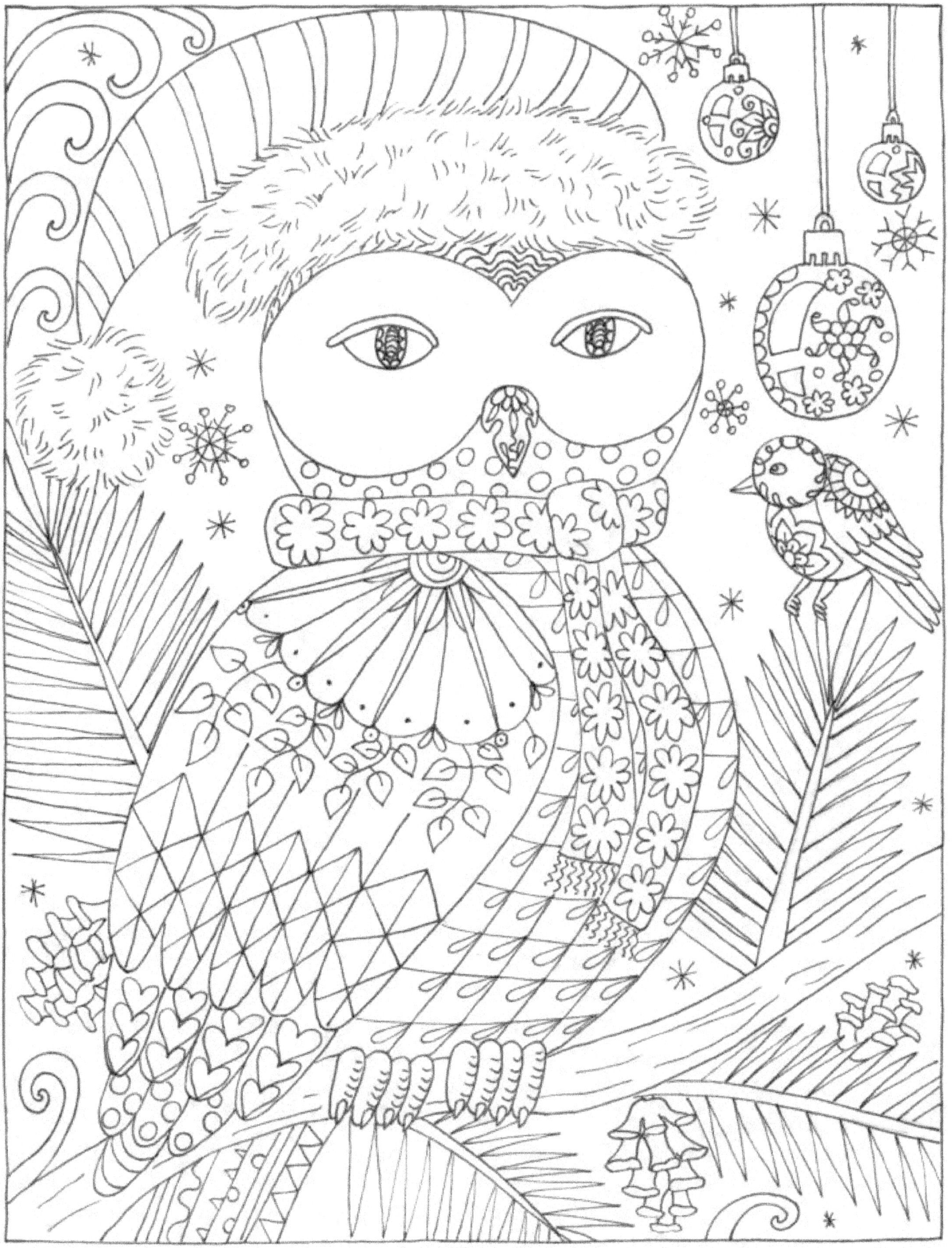

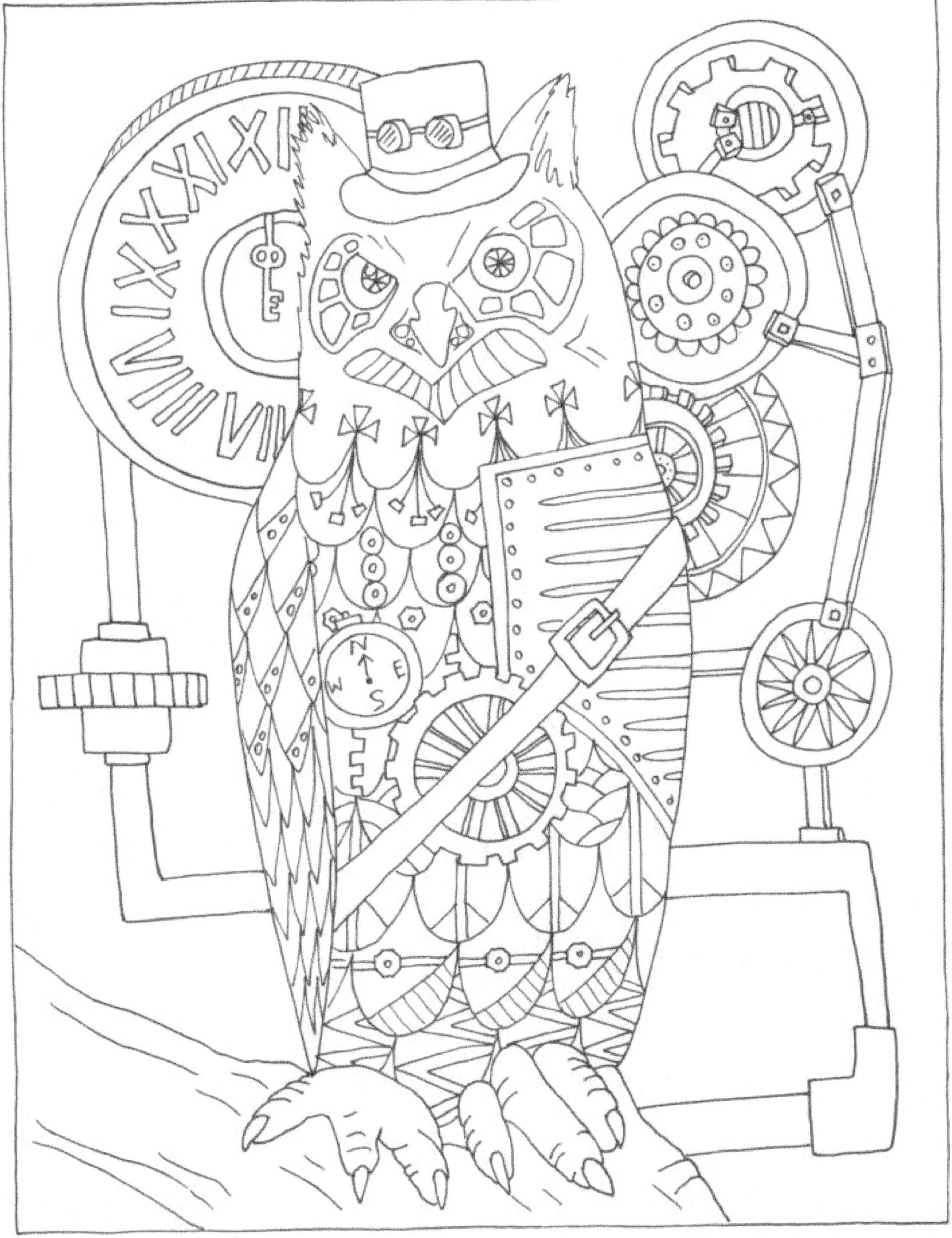
N
E
S
W

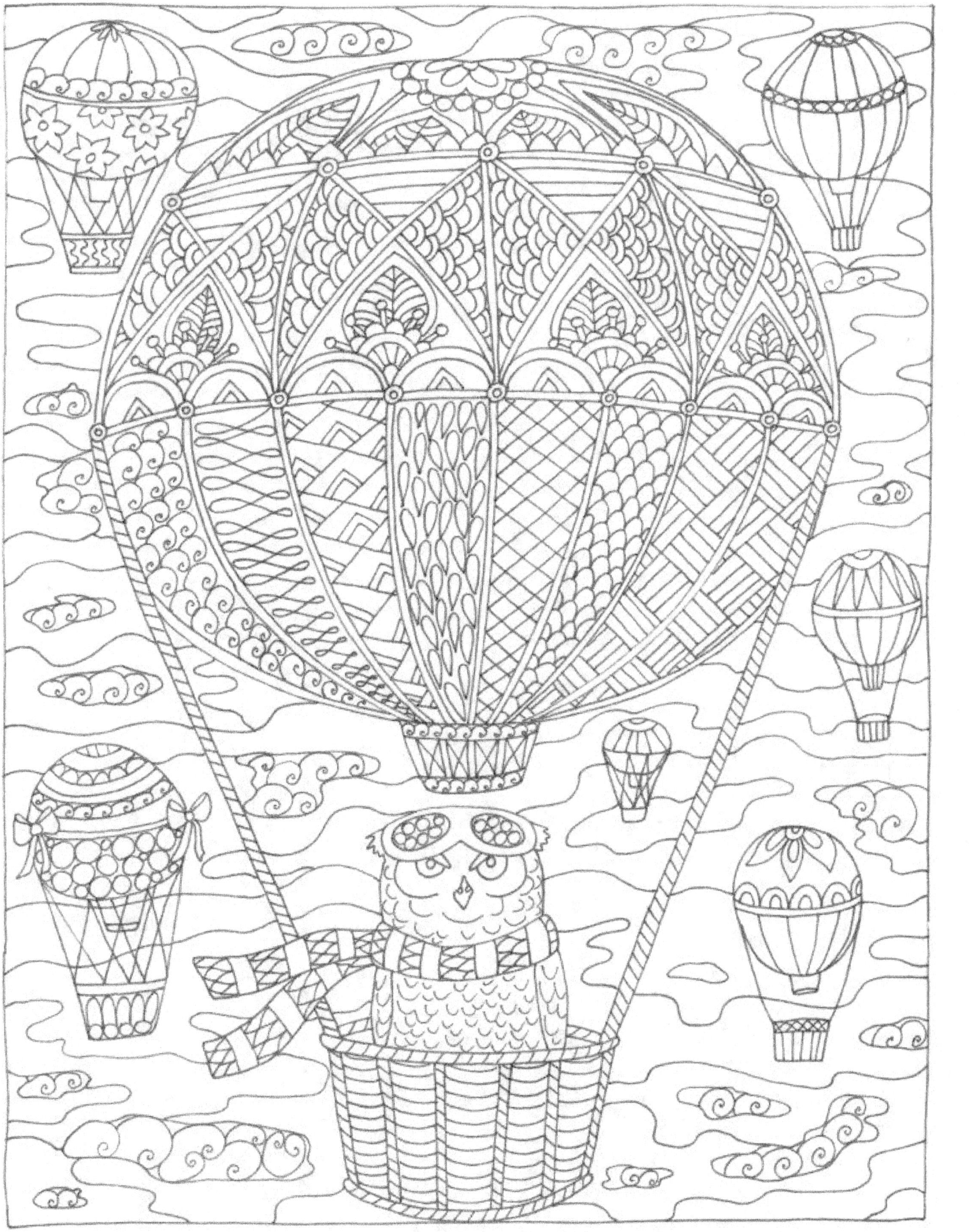

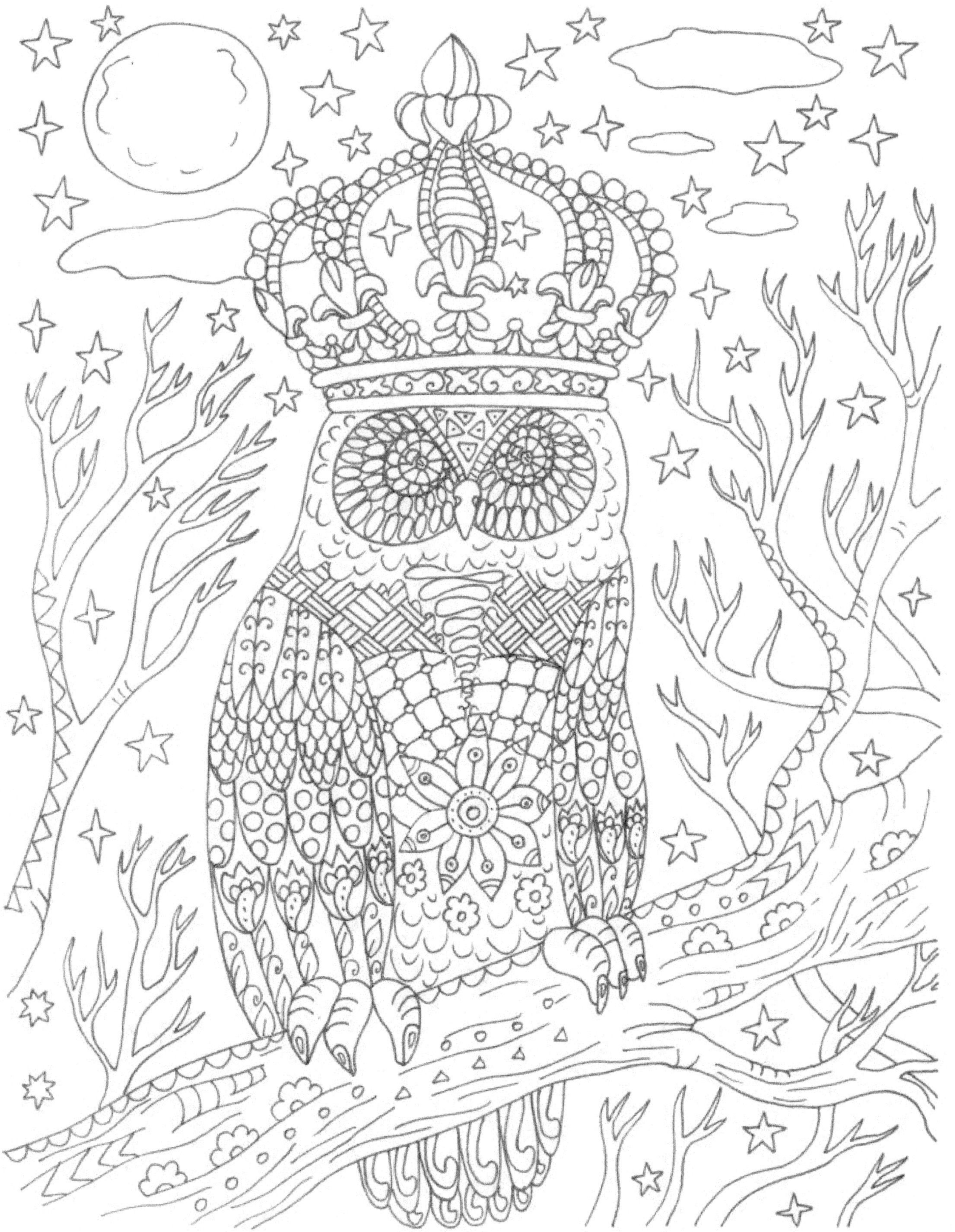